W9-BPK-109

WITHDRAWN

Knowing Yourself, Knowing Others

A Workbook for Children with Asperger's Disorder, Nonverbal Learning Disorder, and Other Social-Skill Problems

Barbara Cooper & Nancy Widdows

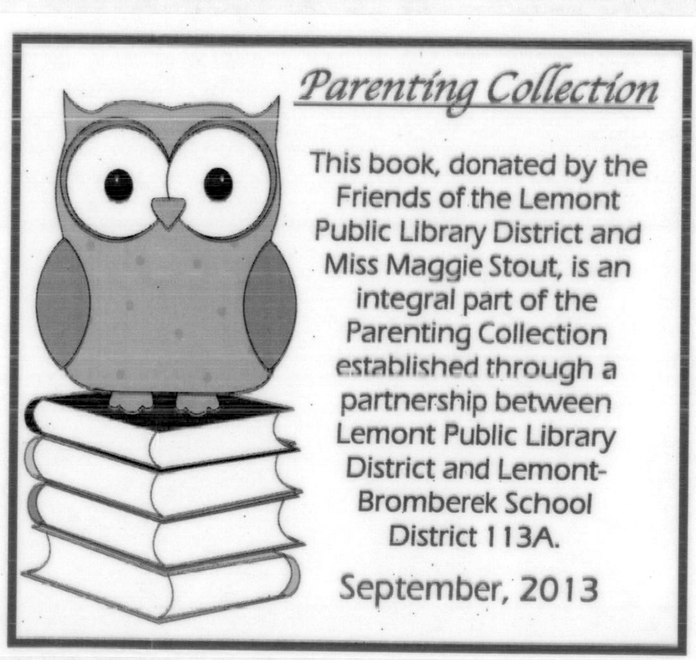
Parenting Collection
This book, donated by the Friends of the Lemont Public Library District and Miss Maggie Stout, is an integral part of the Parenting Collection established through a partnership between Lemont Public Library District and Lemont-Bromberek School District 113A.
September, 2013

LEMONT PUBLIC LIBRARY DISTRICT
50 East Wend Street
Lemont, IL 60439-6439

9/13

Publisher's Note

This publication is designed to provide accurate and authoritative information in regard to the subject matter covered. It is sold with the understanding that the publisher is not engaged in rendering psychological, financial, legal, or other professional services. If expert assistance or counseling is needed, the services of a competent professional should be sought.

Distributed in Canada by Raincoast Books

Copyright © 2008 by Barbara Cooper and Nancy Widdows
Instant Help Books
A Division of New Harbinger Publications, Inc.
5674 Shattuck Avenue
Oakland, CA 94609
www.newharbinger.com

Cover design by Amy Shoup
Illustration by Robin C. Morris

All photographs are models used for illustrative purposes only.

All rights reserved

Printed in the United States of America

Library of Congress Cataloging-in-Publication Data

Cooper, Barbara.
Knowing yourself, knowing others : a workbook for children with Asperger's disorder, nonverbal learning disorder, and other social-skill problems / Barbara Cooper, and Nancy Widdows.
p. cm.
ISBN-13: 978-1-57224-605-8 (pbk. : alk. paper)
ISBN-10: 1-57224-605-7 (pbk. : alk. paper) 1. Asperger's syndrome in children--Patients--Rehabilitation--Problems, exercises, etc. 2. Nonverbal learning disabilities--Patients--Rehabilitation--Problems, exercises, etc. 3. Social skills in children--Study and teaching (Elementary)--Activity programs. I. Widdows, Nancy. II. Title.
RJ506.A9C669 2008
618.92'858832--dc22

2008003635

10 09 08

10 9 8 7 6 5 4 3 2 1

3 1559 00242 6490

Contents

Dear Reader,

This book is full of activities that can help you learn more about yourself and other people. Why is this important? When you understand more about your feelings, the feelings of other people, and how you get along with other people, life becomes easier and more fun. We know this because we help lots of kids learn how to make friends, keep friends, and have more fun with friends. These kids have taught us a lot about what helps and what doesn't, and we're happy to pass this along to you!

A grown-up probably gave you this book. They gave you this book to help you get better at noticing how people feel and act, and to feel better about yourself.

How to Use This Book

The activities in this book go in order. It's important to do them in order so that they will make sense and help you. You can do some of these activities on your own, and for others you will need adult help.

There is a symbol to show you when to ask for help: .

It's always a good idea to share your finished activities with the adult who gave you this book. This can help them to help you. Some of the activities ask you to draw a picture, and it's important for you to know that how you draw doesn't count as long as you are putting down your thoughts and feelings.

You will also find other symbols in the book. These are to help you and the person who gave you the book to know what type of activity it is and how it can help you.

	Communication tool	This tool will help you let others know your thoughts and feelings.
	Investigative tool	This tool will help you pay attention and learn about the people and the world around you.
	Visual tool	This tool will get you to make pictures that help you remember what you've learned.
	Learning tool	This tool will give you information that helps you learn new things.
	Adult assistance needed	This symbol means that an adult needs either to help you find materials for the project or to discuss and explain parts of the activity to you.

We hope that this book helps you and that you have fun doing the activities!

—Nancy and Barbara

A Note to Parents

There are many children who experience problems in relating to others. They may have a nonverbal learning disorder, Asperger's syndrome, or another developmental problem. In some cases, children have no formal diagnosis, and yet they seem to lack empathy, have poor emotional management skills, and struggle with even the most basic social rules. No matter the cause of a child's social-skills problems, this workbook can help.

The emotional, behavioral, and social skills taught in this book follow "best practices" in helping children with social-skills problems, including:

- Breaking tasks down into concrete tasks and skills
- Encouraging self-evaluation and social awareness
- Developing problem-solving strategies
- Reinforcing new, appropriate behaviors

The activities were developed at the coauthors' SuperKids Centers and they were tested with children who have many different social-skill problems. In fact, many of the activities were suggested by the children themselves!

The activities in this book will help you teach children to understand their feelings, develop social confidence, and communicate their social needs in ways that are appropriate to the setting. They will be invaluable skills for all children to learn.

If you have bought this book for a child who has moderate to severe social-skill problems, we urge you to use it in the context of your child's total treatment program, continuing to pursue psychological, medical, and educational help. Consider the workbook as a kind of "psychological homework," using it to help children practice social skills at home and to support the professionals who are working with your child. The activities in this workbook will be most helpful if they are used to reinforce the skills that your child has learned in a peer setting.

As you go over the activities with your child, you will likely find out that it is difficult for him to talk about certain issues. Never force your child to talk if he doesn't want to. The best way to get children to open up is to be a good role model. Talk about your thoughts, feelings, and experiences as they relate to each activity, stressing the positive ways that *you* cope with problems. Even if your child doesn't say a thing back, your words will have an impact on his behavior.

There is no wrong way to use this workbook to help your child, as long as you remain patient and respectful of your child's feelings. If your child is being seen by a counselor, make sure you share this workbook with the therapist. She may have some additional ideas on how best to use the activities.

It is difficult to watch children as they struggle with their social world. No one likes to see children being teased, ignored, or rejected. But have faith that with a concerted effort, along with patience and understanding, these children can learn to relate to others.

Sincerely,

Lawrence E. Shapiro, PhD

Match the Feeling Activity 1

You Need to Know

If you want to know what other people are feeling, you need to look at the clues their faces and bodies give.

Some people are very good at knowing what clues other peoples' faces and bodies are giving that help to show what they are feeling. Other people need to work on this to get good at it.

One way to practice this is to really notice other peoples' faces and bodies when you know what they are feeling. For example, if your mom tells you she is mad, look at her face and her body. What clues do you see? Her mouth might look like a straight line. Her eyebrows might look closer together. Her face might look red. Her voice might get louder. Her body might look stiff.

Try an experiment. Look in a mirror and think of something that makes you angry. How does your mouth look? Your eyebrows? Your body? Even though everyone's face and body might look a little different when they are having a feeling, there are some things that are similar for everyone.

"Facial expression" is another way of saying that your face is giving a clue about the way you are feeling. "Body language" is another way of saying your body is giving a clue about what you are feeling.

Directions

Which facial expression and body language would match your feelings? Draw a line from the situation to the picture that best matches the feeling you would have in that situation.

1. You just found out today that your best friend is moving away.

2. You just got home and found out your mom bought you the game you have wanted for a long time.

3. Your family is planning a trip to an amusement park, and you're very excited. You wake up and it's raining.... You can't go!

4. You start to play your new video game and you are unable to get past level 1.

5. Tomorrow is your birthday, and you will be able to do anything you'd like to do!

6. Tomorrow is the first day of school. You don't know who will be in your class.

7. Someone in your class teased you for a few days. When you yelled for him to stop, you got in trouble with the teacher.

8. There's a math problem on the board in school that you don't know how to solve. Your teacher calls on you to go up to the board and solve the problem in front of the whole class.

Take Note

What facial expression and body language give you clues that someone is sad?

____

____

____

What facial expression and body language give you clues that someone is happy?

____

____

____

What facial expression and body language give you clues that someone is disappointed?

____

____

____

What facial expression and body language give you clues that someone is frustrated?

____

____

____

Activity 2 Comic-Strip Stories

You Need to Know

If you want to know why people feel a certain way in situations, you need to look at all that has happened and at their face and body for clues.

When you try to figure out how someone is feeling, it is important to think about what just happened to them.

For example, your mom might tell you that she is mad, and you can tell by her body and face that she is mad. When you think about what just happened, you realize that there is a mark on the kitchen wall and your baby brother is holding a marker. You remember your mother asking you to keep the markers away from your baby brother. You forgot to pay attention to where you put the markers and you left one on the floor by mistake. Your baby brother must have taken it and written on the wall. Now you know what your mom is mad about.

Directions

Write a story about how the kids are feeling in the following cartoons on the lines provided.

Take Note

Write a few sentences about a situation where you noticed someone feeling mad.

____

____

Did you notice this person was feeling this way by what was happening or by looking for facial expressions and body language, or both? ______________________

Write a few sentences about a situation where you noticed someone feeling disappointed.

____

____

Did you notice this person was feeling this way by what was happening or by looking for facial expressions and body language or both? ______________________

Write a few sentences about a situation where you noticed someone feeling worried.

____

____

Did you notice this person was feeling this way by what was happening or by looking for facial expressions and body language or both? ______________________

Write a few sentences about a situation where you noticed someone feeling excited.

____

____

Feelings Collage: Happy!

> ***You Need to Know***
>
> Learning more about your own feelings can help you understand yourself better. Once you know more about your feelings, it can help you make guesses about how something makes someone else feel.

Different things make different people happy. For example, Joe likes horses and gets excited about going for riding lessons, but Bobby is afraid of horses and would never want to ride one. Thinking about horses makes Joe happy. Thinking about horses makes Bobby worried.

It's important to know what makes you happy and what you look like when you are happy. This way you will know if your face and body are giving the right clues to other people who may be trying to guess how you feel.

It's also important to know that there are different levels of happiness. For example, when people feel a little happy, they might say they are pleased, and when they are VERY happy, they might say they are thrilled. Can you tell by someone's face and body if they are a little happy or very happy?

Activity 3 Feelings Collage: Happy!

Directions

Find pictures in magazines and photos of yourself and people you know that look happy. Cut out and paste these pictures onto this page. Give it a happy title.

Take Note

Looking at your happy collage, write down words that you think match the images you see. How many words can you come up with?

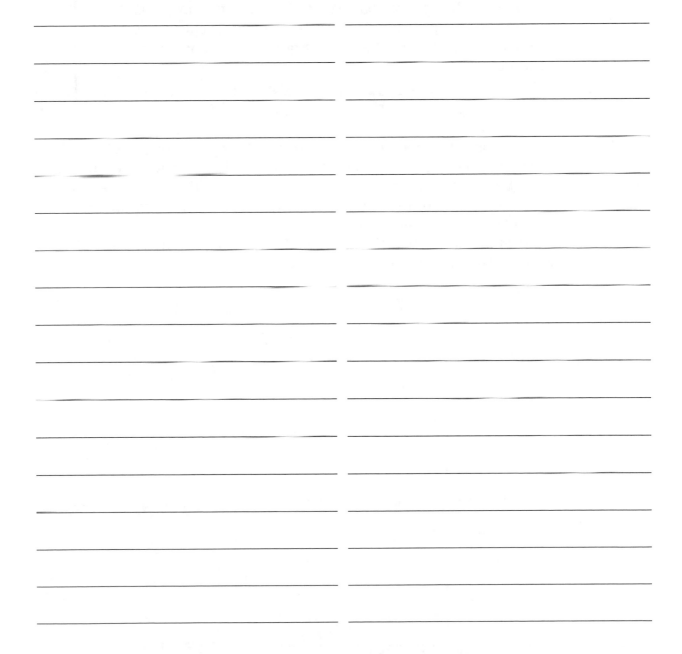

Activity 4 Things That Make Me Happy

You Need to Know

Things that make you happy might be different from things that make other people happy. It's important to know what makes you happy so that you can let other people know. Sometimes this helps other people give you what you need or want.

Susie loves to read and is very good at it. Until last year, Susie's mother would read her a story before bed every night. Once she could read well on her own, her mother stopped doing this. Susie loved spending that time with her mother and misses this bedtime routine. When Susie thinks about what makes her happy, she thinks about that time. Susie told her mother, and her mother was surprised since Susie's such a good reader and likes to read by herself. Susie's mother began reading to Susie at bedtime again. This made both of them very happy.

Things That Make Me Happy

Directions

Find pictures in magazines that show situations or things that make you happy. Cut out and paste these pictures onto this page.

Activity 4 Things That Make Me Happy

Take Note

Now that you have made your collage, write down the things that make you happy below:

____

____

____

If there are any things you listed above that your parents might not know about, list them here:

____

____

____

You may want to share these things with your parents.

Do you have any friends who might list the same things if they were asked about what made them happy?

____

____

____

Feelings Collage: Sad

Activity 5

You Need to Know

Learning more about your own feelings can help you understand yourself better. Once you know more about your feelings it can help you make guesses about how something makes someone else feel.

Different things make different people sad. For example, when Lily goes to school, she gets very sad because she has to leave her mother. She even cries sometimes. Will loves to go to school and does not feel sad about leaving his mother.

It's important to know what makes you sad and what you look like when you are sad. This way you will know if your face and body are giving the right clues to other people who may be trying to guess how you feel.

It's also important to know that there are different levels of sadness. For example, when people feel a little sad, they might say they are gloomy and when they are VERY sad, they might say they are miserable. Can you tell by someone's face and body if they are a little sad or very sad?

Feelings Collage: Sad

Directions

Find pictures in magazines and find photos of yourself and people you know who look sad. Cut out and paste these pictures onto this page. Give it a sad title.

Take Note

Looking at your sad collage, write down words that you think match the faces in your collage. How many words can you come up with?

Activity 6 Things That Make Me Sad

You Need to Know

Things that make you sad might be different from things that make other people sad. It's important to know what makes you sad so that you can let other people know. Sometimes this helps other people give you what you need or want.

Jared's dad goes away on business trips. Jared misses his dad when he is away. He especially misses talking to him in the morning when he wakes up, because Jared's dad usually wakes him up in the morning and they talk about the day ahead. When Jared thinks about what makes him sad, he thinks about missing his dad in the morning. When Jared tells his dad about this, his father is glad to know this because even though he knew Jared missed him, he didn't know that it was the mornings when he missed him most. Jared's dad began calling him in the morning when he was away on business trips. This made everyone happy.

Directions

Find pictures in magazines that show situations or things that make you sad. Cut out and paste these pictures onto this page.

Take Note

Now that you have made your collage, write down the things that make you sad below:

____

____

____

If there are any things you listed above that your parents might not know about, list them here:

____

____

____

You may want to share these things with your parents.

Do you have any friends who might list the same things if they were asked about what made them sad?

____

____

____

Feelings Collage: Worried

Activity 7

You Need to Know

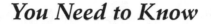

Learning more about your own feelings can help you understand yourself better. Once you know more about your feelings, it can help you make guesses about how something makes someone else feel.

Different things make different people worried. For example, Christian becomes worried when he is about to go somewhere new. Sam loves to go to new places and gets excited about it.

It's important to know what makes you worried and what you look like when you are worried. This way you will know if your face and body are giving the right clues to other people who may be trying to guess how you feel.

Directions

Find pictures in magazines and find photos of yourself and people you know who look worried. Cut out and paste these pictures onto this page. Give it a worried title.

Take Note

Looking at your worried collage, write down words that you think match the faces in your collage. How many words can you come up with?

Activity 8 Things That Make Me Worried

You Need to Know

Things that make you worried might be different from things that make other people worried. It's important to know what makes you worried so that you can let other people know. Sometimes this helps other people give you what you need or want.

Amanda worried every day before she had to get on the school bus. Every day a girl named Missy picked on Amanda by calling her names. Amanda took too long to get ready so that she would miss the school bus. Amanda's mother got very angry at Amanda, and they were always arguing about it.

When Amanda thought about what made her worried, she realized seeing Missy on the bus was a big worry. Amanda was then able to tell her mother about this, and her mother understood why Amanda took too long to get ready. She was happy that Amanda told her so that she could do something about it.

Directions

Find pictures in magazines that show situations or things that make you worried. Cut out and paste these pictures onto this page.

Take Note

Now that you have made your collage, write down the things that make you worried below:

____

____

____

If there are any things you listed above that your parents might not know about, list them here:

____

____

____

You may want to share these things with your parents.

Do you have any friends who might list the same things if they were asked about what made them worried?

____

____

____

Feelings Collage: Angry

Activity 9

You Need to Know

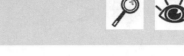

Learning more about your own feelings can help you understand yourself better. Once you know more about your feelings, it can help you make guesses about how something makes someone else feel.

Different things make different people angry. For example, when Adam loses a game he gets very angry. He even throws the game board sometimes. Dylan doesn't mind losing a game. He knows he has a chance to win next time.

It's important to know what makes you angry and what you look like when you are angry. This way you will know if your face and body are giving the right clues to other people who may be trying to guess how you feel.

It's also important to know that there are different levels of anger. For example, when people feel a little angry, they might say they are annoyed and when they are VERY angry, they might say they are furious. Can you tell by someone's face and body if they are a little angry or very angry?

Directions

Find pictures in magazines and find photos of yourself and people you know who look angry. Cut out and paste these pictures onto this page. Give it an angry title.

Take Note

Looking at your angry collage, write down words that you think match the faces in your collage. How many words can you come up with?

Activity 10 Things That Make Me Angry

You Need to Know

Things that make you angry might be different from things that make other people angry. It's important to know what makes you angry so that you can let other people know. Sometimes this helps other people give you what you need or want.

In the car, after school, Luke always sat next to his younger sister. She loved to sing, especially in the car. The sound of her singing would annoy Luke so much that he would hit her to make her stop. Their mother, who was driving the car, would blame Luke for being mean to his sister. She didn't know that the singing made Luke furious. When Luke thought about what made him angry in the car, he realized that it was his sister's singing. He was then able to tell his mother about this, and his mother realized the reason Luke was hitting his sister. She was happy that Luke told her so that she could help.

Things That Make Me Angry

Directions

Find pictures in magazines that show situations or things that make you angry. Cut out and paste these pictures onto this page.

Take Note

Now that you have made your collage, write down the things that make you angry below:

____

____

____

If there are any things you listed above that your parents might not know about, list them here:

____

____

____

You may want to share these things with your parents.

Do you have any friends who might list the same things if they were asked about what made them angry?

____

____

____

Different Kinds of Anger Activity 11

You Need to Know

There are many different kinds of anger. Knowing about the different levels of anger can help you know how you feel about things that happen to you.

Kristen gets annoyed when the boy that sits next to her in her class is tapping his pencil on his desk while she is trying to work. When Kristen is annoyed, her voice sometimes gets loud and she uses words that are not friendly.

Kristen gets mad when her mother tells her she can't watch her favorite TV show because she did not finish her homework. When Kristen is mad, she yells, and sometimes her yelling leads to crying.

Some kids, even when they are just bothered, become VERY angry. This can be confusing and scary to other kids. You might have had a situation where people around you told you that you were "overreacting" and that there was "nothing to be mad about."

We hope this activity will help you to understand that there are different kinds of anger.

Activity 11 Different Kinds of Anger

If you look back at your collage of what makes you angry, you can see that some things make you feel a little angry and other things might make you feel VERY angry. In Activity 10, you were asked to write words that describe anger. Look at our list below and rearrange the words so the word at the top of the list would be the least angry and the word at the bottom of the list would be the most angry.

Annoyed ____________________

Mad ____________________

Furious ____________________

Upset ____________________

Frustrated ____________________

Bothered ____________________

Read the following stories. Match each story to an angry word from the list above.

1. Jamie wants to play chess, but Andy wants to play a different game. Andy refuses to play chess, even though Jamie really wants to play. How might Jamie feel? ____________________
2. Sarah is trying to do her math homework and is getting all the answers wrong. No matter how much she tries, she just doesn't get it. How might Sarah feel? ____________________
3. Bobby is in the back seat of the car with his little brother, and his little brother is poking him with a straw even though Bobby has asked him to stop. How might Bobby feel? ____________________
4. Brandon is outside at recess. He goes up to a group of boys playing tag and asks if he can play. Brandon begins to play and because he can't run very fast, he always loses. The other kids tease him about how slow he is. How might Brandon feel? ____________________
5. Samantha is going to her ballet class. She likes to be the first one in the room so that she can get the spot by the mirror that she likes before anyone else takes it. On this day, Samantha is late and ends up being the last one in the room. How might Samantha feel? ____________________

Take Note

Now that you've learned about the different levels of anger, you can answer some questions:

Think about a time when you felt annoyed. What was it that annoyed you?

What do you do when you are annoyed?

Think about a time when your mom felt annoyed. What was it that annoyed her? (If you can't think of an example, ask her.)

What does she do when she is annoyed?

Think about a time when you felt angry. What was it that angered you?

What do you do when you are angry?

____

____

____

Think about a time when your dad felt angry. What was it that angered him? (If you can't think of an example, ask him.)

____

____

____

What does he do when he is angry?

____

____

____

Where Do I Feel These Feelings in My Body?

Activity 12

You Need to Know

When you feel a feeling, you might think about it in your head. At the same time, you feel it in your body too. Some people are good at knowing how a feeling makes their body feel. Some people need to learn and practice knowing this. If you can get good at this, it will help you pay attention to your feelings before they get too big.

James plays the flute in the school band. Tomorrow is the concert and James has to play a part of one song all by himself. He is thinking that he might make a mistake while he is playing in front of all the people who will be there to see the concert. James has been thinking about the concert all day, and he has a stomachache and his leg is jiggling up and down while he is thinking. James needs to learn that when he has a stomachache and his legs are jiggly, he is worried. Once he knows this, he can help himself to feel less worried.

Activity 12

Where Do I Feel These Feelings in My Body?

Directions

Pick a body outline to color. Think about something that makes you feel the feeling written below the outline. Stand and make your body into the position that you take when you have this feeling. Color the areas inside the body outline where you feel this feeling the most. For example, if you ball your hands into fists when you are angry, color in the hands of the body outline.

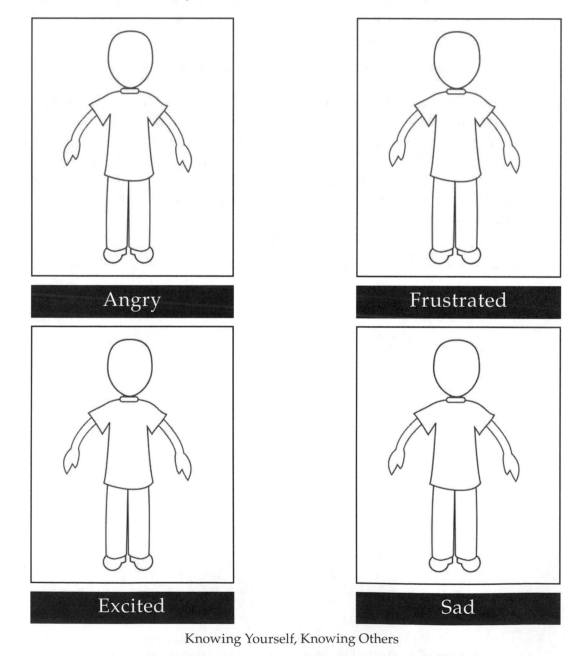

Angry

Frustrated

Excited

Sad

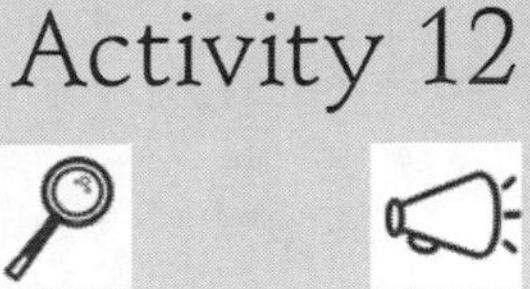

Take Note

Now that you've colored in the outlines, you can answer some questions:

Where in your body do you feel anger?

____

Do you think you notice this when it is happening?

Yes ____________ No ___________

If yes, it might be helpful to tell a grown-up when you are feeling this way.

If no, it might be helpful for you and your parent to talk about what you feel like inside when you are angry and what your face and body look like. Then your parent can look for these clues and tell you when he or she thinks you might be angry so you can check your body to see if you are feeling this way. This will help you learn to notice your feeling all by yourself.

Where in your body do you feel frustrated?

____

Do you think you notice this when it is happening?

Yes ____________ No ___________

If yes, it might be helpful to tell a grown-up when you are feeling this way.

If no, it might be helpful for you and your parent to talk about what you feel like inside when you are frustrated and what your face and body look like. Then your parent can look for these clues and tell you when he or she thinks you might be frustrated so you can check your body to see if you are feeling this way. This will help you learn to notice your feeling all by yourself.

Where Do I Feel These Feelings in My Body?

Where in your body do you feel excited?

____

Do you think you notice this when it is happening?

Yes __________ No __________

If yes, it might be helpful to tell a grown-up when you are feeling this way.

If no, it might be helpful for you and your parent to talk about what you feel like inside when you are excited and what your face and body look like. Then your parent can look for these clues and tell you when he or she thinks you might be excited so you can check your body to see if you are feeling this way. This will help you learn to notice your feeling all by yourself.

Where in your body do you feel sad?

____

Do you think you notice this when it is happening?

Yes __________ No __________

If yes, it might be helpful to tell a grown-up when you are feeling this way.

If no, it might be helpful for you and your parent to talk about what you feel like inside when you are sad and what your face and body look like. Then your parent can look for these clues and tell you when he or she thinks you might be sad so you can check your body to see if you are feeling this way. This will help you learn to notice your feeling all by yourself.

You Need to Know

Some people are really good at knowing what they are feeling and some people need to learn how to do this. The paint-chip key chain is a tool to help you know what you are feeling at a particular time.

Katie was having a hard time at school. She didn't really know why, but every day when she was doing her work right before lunchtime, she would get a little upset. If someone, like her teacher, asked her if something was wrong, she would cry. Everyone asked her to explain why she was upset, but Katie just didn't know what to say. She was confused and upset.

Katie's school counselor knew that Katie learned better when someone explained something to her in pictures instead of just words. Her counselor knew that using colors to match feelings might help Katie know what she was feeling. Together they made a paint-chip key chain. She practiced using it at home and in school when she wasn't upset. This taught her to pay attention to what she was feeling when things were okay. When she got upset before lunch one day she took out the key chain and really thought about what she was feeling. She picked the color chip for "sad." When her teacher asked her why she was sad, Katie was able to explain that she used to sit with her friend Beth last year at lunch every day. They liked each other a lot and had fun at lunch. This year she couldn't sit with Beth because they were in different classes. This made her sad.

Activity 13 Paint-Chip Key Chain

Directions

How to make your paint-chip key chain. Have a grownup get paint-chip samples from the hardware store in a large variety of colors. Make sure that you have at least one shade of blue, red, yellow, orange, green, purple, white, and black.

Pick a paint-chip color for each of the following feelings: happy, sad, angry, frustrated, scared or worried, excited, lonely, overwhelmed, surprised, calm, and shy. You can add any other feelings that you think you feel a lot.

Cut the paint chip into a small square or rectangular shape and punch a hole with a hole puncher into one of the corners of the color. Label the back of the chip with the feeling you chose.

Take a key ring or a piece of string and connect the chips.

Here's how to use your paint-chip key chain. Carry the key chain in your pocket so that you have it with you at all times. Experiment with using it at different times. When you have any type of strong feeling, take the key chain out and find the paint chip that best matches what you are feeling. Notice how your body is feeling at that time. For example, some people who are angry make fists with their hands and hold them tight or jiggle their legs when they are worried.

When you are not having a strong feeling, take the key chain out and find the paint chip that best matches your feeling. Notice how your body is feeling at that time.

When you are confused about how you are feeling, take the key chain out and find the feeling chip that best describes what you might be feeling. Remember that it may be possible to be feeling two different feelings at the same time and that may be what's confusing to you.

Practice using the paint-chip key chain and see if you get better at knowing and paying attention to what you are feeling. If there is a grown-up who can practice this with you at home, it would be good for them to use the key chain too so that you can notice what someone else looks like (their body and their face) when they have a particular feeling.

Take Note

How many colors did you use for your key chain?

___

Were you able to use different shades of a color for different shades of a feeling?

___

Please share an example of this:

___

When do you think this might be helpful to you? List some situations where you are confused about your feelings.

___

___

___

___

Write about a time where you used your key chain and it helped you.

___

___

___

___

Activity 14 Something Happened to Me Today

You Need to Know

People who spend time together can have different feelings about what happens when they are together. It's important to know that other people might have a different way of thinking about and seeing what's going on.

Spencer was playing chess with Bobby. Spencer had only played chess a few times before. Bobby played chess with his dad all the time and was quite good at it. Halfway through the game, when Spencer was stuck and unable to make a move, Bobby offered to help by teaching Spencer some strategies that he thought Spencer didn't know. Spencer was frustrated and became angry when Bobby tried to help, thinking that Bobby was really trying to tell Spencer to make a bad move so that he could win. Bobby got upset because he was just trying to help and didn't like being accused of cheating.

Even though Spencer and Bobby were together, they were having different thoughts and feelings about what was happening.

Directions

Draw something that happened to you today, when you were with other kids, that might include one of these feelings:

Frustration, excitement, disappointment, hope, worry, loneliness, being left out.

What do you think the other kid or kids might have been feeling? Draw a picture to describe this.

Take Note

Write about your first drawing. Include what happened and how you felt.

Write about your second drawing. Tell how the other person might have felt.

Share these drawings and what you wrote with your parents and/or with the adult who gave you this book.

You Need to Know

We all have many parts to who we are. Some people are really good at some things and not so good at others. Thinking about your strengths and weaknesses will help you know that you are good at some things while you are working on getting better at what's hard for you.

Val has been able to read since she was three years old. Now in the third grade, Val is the best reader in the class. At recess, however, Val has a hard time because the noise and crowds of kids get her confused and she doesn't know where to go or what to do. She often spends recess alone. So Val's strength is reading, and her weakness is recess.

Val would love to enjoy recess like the other kids seem to do. She gets frustrated because she doesn't know how to do this. The school counselor noticed that Val was often by herself in the schoolyard. She offered to help Val learn how to deal with the noise and the crowds. At first Val was embarrassed to get this help because she thought she should know how to do this. Nobody else seemed to need this kind of help. Val didn't know that some of the kids that were great at recess needed help with reading. Everybody has strengths and weaknesses!

Directions

Think about some of your strengths and weaknesses. Draw a picture below that shows at least one of each. If you have trouble with this, ask an adult who knows you well for help.

Take Note

What strengths do you think you have? What are you good at?

____

____

____

How do you know this?

____

____

____

What weaknesses do you think you have? What do you struggle with?

____

____

____

How do you know this?

____

____

____

Activity 16 Something About Myself I Would Never Change/Something I Would Like to Change

You Need to Know

We all have many parts to who we are. Some people are really good at some things, and not so good at others. Thinking about your strengths and weaknesses will help you know that you are good at some things while you are working on getting better at what's hard for you.

Justin is really great at using a computer. He knows more about computers than most other kids. He is great at helping kids in his class with the computer. He is proud of being able to do this. It's a part of himself that he would never change.

When it's time for recess, Justin has trouble finding other kids to play with. He wanders around the schoolyard alone. He feels lonely and frustrated that other kids don't seem to like to play with him. Justin is not so great at recess. It's something he would love to change.

Something About Myself I Would Never Change/Something I Would Like to Change

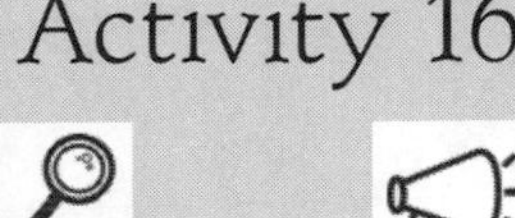

Activity 16

Directions

Draw a picture and/or write about this: something that I really like about myself and that I would never want to change.

Draw a picture and/or write about this: something about myself that I don't like and wish I could change.

Activity 16

Something About Myself I Would Never Change/Something I Would Like to Change

Take Note

What aspect of yourself did you draw about that you would never change?

____

____

____

Why? ____

____

____

What aspect of yourself did you draw about that you would like to change?

____

____

____

Why? ____

____

____

What aspect of yourself do you think your parents would like you to change?

____

____

____

Why? ____

____

____

Something About Myself I Would Never Change/Something I Would Like to Change

What aspect of yourself do you think your teacher would like you to change?

____

____

____

Why? ____________________________________

____

____

Share your drawings and writing with your parents and/or the adult who gave you this book. They may be able to help you find ways to work on what you'd like to change.

Activity 17 Feelings Checklist

You Need to Know

Sometimes kids have a hard time telling other people what they feel during their day. It's important to be able to let your parents or other important people know how you feel when they are not around. Doing this checklist will also help you pay attention to your feelings.

When kids don't tell parents or other important people what's happening, sometimes feelings build up inside (like a volcano) and one day, without even knowing it, they can explode.

Alex sat in the back of his classroom next to a boy named Zachary. Every day, Zachary would call Alex names. Zachary did it in a low voice so that he wouldn't get in trouble. Alex did not tell anybody about what was going on for months. He tried to forget about it. One day, Zachary called Alex a name, and Alex picked up a chair and threw it at Zachary. Alex's anger, which he tried to forget about, had built up to a point where it caused him to react in a way he normally wouldn't.

Alex learned to use this checklist as a way to make sure his parents and important people in school (teacher, counselor) knew what was going on for him, how he felt, and if there were any situations with other kids that they needed to help him with.

The story about Alex shows a situation that got out of control. This checklist is a way to prevent an explosion. It is also a way to share all kinds of feelings that you felt during your day, both good and bad.

It is good practice to help you pay attention to your feelings.

To use this checklist, make copies of the blank one on the next page.

Directions

Circle the phrase that best describes how often you felt the following today:

HAPPY	Not at all	A little	A lot	All the Time
SAD	Not at all	A little	A lot	All the Time
FRUSTRATED	Not at all	A little	A lot	All the Time
LONELY	Not at all	A little	A lot	All the Time
INCLUDED	Not at all	A little	A lot	All the Time
ANGRY	Not at all	A little	A lot	All the Time
LEFT OUT / DIFFERENT	Not at all	A little	A lot	All the Time
SHY	Not at all	A little	A lot	All the Time
HURT	Not at all	A little	A lot	All the Time
EMBARRASSED	Not at all	A little	A lot	All the Time
HOPEFUL	Not at all	A little	A lot	All the Time
SURPRISED	Not at all	A little	A lot	All the Time
WORRIED	Not at all	A little	A lot	All the Time
I LISTENED TO OTHERS …	Not at all	A little	A lot	All the Time
I ACTED IN WAYS I REGRETTED …	Not at all	A little	A lot	All the Time
I ASKED TO JOIN OTHERS …	Not at all	A little	A lot	All the Time
I FELT I HAD TO IGNORE MY FEELINGS …	Not at all	A little	A lot	All the Time

Take Note

Did using the feelings checklist help you tell someone else about your day?

____

____

After filling out a checklist at the end of a day, did any of your answers surprise you?

Yes __________ No __________

If yes, what surprised you?

____

____

____

Would you do anything differently tomorrow because of how you felt about something today?

Yes __________ No __________

If yes, what would you do?

____

____

____

Are there any feelings you would add to this checklist? If so, what are they?

____

____

Do You Melt Down? Activity 18

You Need to Know

The term "meltdown" is used to describe the state that kids sometimes enter when they are very upset and can't calm themselves. Sometimes people use the word "tantrum" to describe this state. Nobody likes to melt down, but for some people it's just what happens when they get overwhelmed.

This activity is designed to help you find out what might trigger a meltdown, (it's different for everyone), so that you and the grownups around you can know when it's starting to happen and figure out ways to stop it before it happens.

For example, Jessica seems to melt down right before she has to leave the house for school. Her mom is telling her to do lots of things at once ("pack your homework in the backpack," "get your shoes on," "brush your hair" and Jessica becomes overwhelmed and confused about what to do first. Jessica starts yelling and crying and can't stop.

If Jessica and her mom could understand why hearing all these directions at once is hard for Jessica, they could stop the meltdown before it happens. After Jessica does the following activity she and her mom can come up with a better way to start their day.

Directions

Draw a picture of yourself having a meltdown.

Take Note

Think about your picture. Write three things that happened right before your meltdown.

1. ______________________________

2. ______________________________

3. ______________________________

Take out your paint-chip key chain and list the feelings that you were having during each of these three times.

1. ______________________________

2. ______________________________

3. ______________________________

Bring this activity to an adult who can help you understand why the meltdown might have happened. Together you can come up with a way to do something different that changes what happened right before the meltdown. For example, Jessica and her mom came up with the idea to list all of the things that Jessica needs to do before she leaves for school. The list is hung up in Jessica's room and has photos that help remind her to pack her backpack, brush her hair, and put on her shoes. Jessica no longer gets confused by her mom telling her to do too many things at once. And best of all, Jessica no longer melts down before she goes to school!

Write down any new ideas you come up with to avoid a meltdown.

____

____

Do you melt down at home? Yes ____________ No ____________

Do you melt down at school? Yes ____________ No ____________

Name some other places that you meltdown.

____

____

Activity 19 When I Am Angry

You Need to Know

Some kids don't know why people get angry at them. They also might not know why they get angry at other people. Being aware of what you do to make others angry and what they do to make you angry can help you make and keep friends.

Story 1

Rachel doesn't like it when people break the rules. When Ethan got up to sharpen his pencil without asking, she told the teacher. At recess that day, Ethan told the other kids not to play with Rachel because she is a tattletale. The other kids listened to Ethan. Rachel was confused because she thought she had done the right thing in the classroom and she didn't understand why Ethan was so mad and why the other kids couldn't see that she had done the right thing. What Rachel didn't realize was that kids don't like it when you tell on them and that by telling on Ethan she was getting involved in something that had nothing to do with her.

Story 2

Greg gets angry when he wants to play a game with his own rules and the other kids don't want to play that way. One day on the playground he joined a game of tag, insisting that the only way you were "out" was to be tagged three times instead of once. The other kids refused to play this way and continued playing the way they had been. Greg had a meltdown. Greg became angry when he didn't get his way.

Directions

Draw a picture of something you do that makes other people angry.

When I Am Angry

Draw a picture of something that other people do that makes you angry.

Take Note

For drawing 1:

How do other people feel or what do they think when they see you do what you drew about?

____

____

Do you think there's a way that you could change what you do?

Yes __________ No __________

If yes, what could you do differently so that others wouldn't be so mad at you?

____

____

For drawing 2:

Why do you think the person is doing what they are doing?

____

____

Are you able to let the other person know that you are angry?

Yes __________ No __________

If yes, how do you let them know?

____

____

Activity 20 When Plans Change

You Need to Know

Some kids have a hard time when they think something is going to happen in a certain way and then it doesn't go the way they thought it would. It is as if they have a picture in their head and really want that picture to become what happens. When things don't go your way, it's important to realize that plans change for many different reasons.

Adam expects his mom to pick him up from school and take him to the toy store. He is very excited and has thought about it all day. Mom drives up and tells Adam they have to go to the doctor's office because Adam's sister is sick. Adam thinks that they should still be able to go to the toy store. Mom tells Adam that his sister is really sick and needs to go to the doctor right away and that maybe they could go to the toy store another time. Adam begs his mom to keep her promise about the toy store. Mom raises her voice and tells Adam to get into the car right away. Adam refuses and drops his book bag and begins to yell.

Below are some things that might happen next.

1. Adam stays outside of the car, continues screaming for fifteen minutes, and still doesn't get to go to the toy store. Mom is so angry she takes his computer time away for the week.
2. Adam picks up his book bag, still crying, and gets into the car, knowing that he isn't going to the toy store today.
3. Adam's mom gets out of the car and pulls Adam into the car, while other kids from his class are watching.
4. Adam looks at his sister, realizes how sick she is, picks up his book bag, and gets into the car.

Even though Adam is not getting to do what he thought he would be doing that day, which ending would be the best for him?

#1 ____________ #2 ____________ #3 ____________ #4 ____________

Why did you choose the one you did?

____

____

____

____

____

Take Note

Write about a time at home when you couldn't change the plan in your head.

Write about a time at school when you couldn't change the plan in your head.

Changing the Plan in Your Head

Activity 21

You Need to Know

Sometimes having a picture in your mind of what you need to do to deal with unexpected events can help you change the plan in your head. Dealing with unexpected events in a calmer, less upsetting way will help you handle change and avoid meltdowns.

In the previous activity, Adam experienced a change of plan. When the plans change, lots of kids who find this really hard have a meltdown. One of the things you can do is to think about changing the plan in your head. This makes it easier for you to handle unexpected events.

Look at the picture below. The next time something unexpected comes up and you have to change your plan, try to think of this picture, and see if it will help you.

Directions

Think about a time when something unexpected happened to you and you had to change your plan. Write this down here:

____

____

____

____

Now, using the "change the plan" drawing as a guide, draw yourself changing the plan in the situation you just wrote about.

Take Note

Do you think when something unexpected happens, you could remember this picture?

Yes ___________ No ___________

If yes, try it out. Write about what happened after you tried it.

____

____

____

If no, you may want to copy either our picture or yours to keep with you to remember to use it. It's helpful to ask adults in your life to remind you to use it. Who do you think you could share this with?

____

____

Is there a way that you could ask your teacher at school for help with this?

Yes ___________ No ___________

If no, why not?

____

____

____

Keeping a copy of the picture in your desk might be a good way to remember that you can change the plan so that you don't become upset.

Activity 22

Cool-Down Tools: A Safe Place

You Need to Know

A cool-down tool is something you can do to calm yourself down. Many kids think that when they are upset, there's nothing that can help, but we know that there are different ways of calming down that you can learn. Your job is to try them out and find the ones that work for you. This first tool, "A safe place," is a cool-down tool that asks you to use your imagination.

At bedtime, Jenna often thought about all the difficult things that happened to her during the day. This made it really hard for her to fall asleep. She would actually become more and more awake as she thought about these unpleasant things. Jenna learned to imagine a safe place. Her counselor asked her to think of a real place or an imaginary place where everything would be just perfect for Jenna. Jenna remembered her playhouse when she was little. She always felt safe when she was there. The counselor helped her remember exactly what it felt like to be there. This way, Jenna could close her eyes and imagine herself in that playhouse. This helped Jenna to relax, not think about her day, and fall asleep.

Directions

Draw a picture of your favorite safe place. It can be a place that you have been to, a place you'd like to go to, or a place from your imagination. Give the place a name.

As you look at your picture, try to imagine what it would be like to really be there. In addition to what it would look like, what would it smell like there? What would the air feel like there?

___

___

___

___

When something is upsetting you, you can always visit this place in your imagination. This can be a good way to calm down.

Take Note

Different cool-down tools work for different kids. It's important for you to figure out which ones work for you so that you can use them.

Were you able to imagine a safe place?

Yes ___________ No ___________

If no, try a different cool-down tool. The following activities give you more tools to try.

If yes, describe a situation where you used your safe place.

____

____

____

____

Did it help?

Yes ___________ No ___________

Cool-Down Tools: Deep Breaths

Activity 23

You Need to Know

Slow, deep breathing is an automatic way to calm down. When most people become upset, their breathing becomes fast and shallow. Changing your breathing is a great way to cool down anywhere, anytime.

Connor loved baseball and played on a team every Saturday. He would get upset if he didn't play well. Connor was in the outfield when a slow, high fly-ball came his way. He was sure he could catch it. At the last minute, Connor took his eye off the ball and missed the catch. Once he had thrown the ball back to the infield, he knew he felt like he wanted to cry but also knew that this would be very embarrassing. Connor remembered learning how to take slow, deep breaths to calm himself. He did this for a minute or two and was able to continue playing without crying.

Directions

Slow, deep breathing can help you calm down when you are upset. Try the following:

> Lay down on the floor or on your bed and put a book on your tummy. As you breathe in through your nose, the book should gently rise up. As you breathe out through your mouth, your tummy should flatten out, and you will see the book go down. Do this very slowly (or you'll get dizzy!). Do this five times to see how calm you can feel. It might be fun to try this with other people in your family.

Note: doing this breathing exercise along with picturing your safe place will help you calm down even more.

Take Note

Were you able to breathe deeply?

Yes ____________ No ____________

If no, ask someone for help. Learning how to do this can be harder than it seems!

If yes, describe a situation where you used breathing to calm yourself down.

____

____

____

____

Did it help?

Yes ____________ No ____________

List places where you think you can use this cool-down tool.

____

____

____

____

Note: The more you practice this cool-down tool, the more your body will do this all by itself without you even thinking about it!

Activity 24 Cool-Down Tools: Draw a Picture, Write About What You're Feeling

You Need to Know

Some kids, when they are having difficult feelings, keep them a secret. They think that if they ignore these feelings, they will go away. What usually happens, however, is that the feelings get bigger and bigger and become more upsetting over time. Although telling someone about how you feel is always a great idea, sometimes it's not possible. At those times, drawing a picture or writing about how you feel can be a great cool-down tool.

Sean loved to play video games. He often played with his little brother, who was not as good at playing them as he was. Sean sometimes got frustrated when his brother seemed to be ignoring Sean's advice on how to be a better player. This would often lead to a fight. Sean's counselor helped him make a book where he could draw his feelings. Sean found that if he drew out his feelings of frustration about his brother, he would be calmer the next time he had to deal with him while playing videos. If Sean wanted to, he could share these drawings with his counselor, or he could keep them private.

It's helpful to have a sketchbook or journal that you can easily find so that when something is upsetting you, you can find the book and draw a picture or write about what's happening to make you feel this way. You might be surprised at how helpful this can be!

Cool Down Tools: Draw a Picture, Write About What You're Feeling

Directions

In the space below, for practice, draw and/or write about something that has happened to you today that made you angry. You might also want to write about what you drew.

Take Note

Did your feelings change as a result of drawing and/or writing?

Yes ___________ No ___________

If no, try a different cool down tool.

If yes, describe how your feelings changed.

____

____

List places where you think you can use this cool-down tool.

List places where you think you can't use this cool-down tool. (For example, some teachers will let you draw during class and some won't. If you are not allowed to do this at school, try a different cool-down tool.)

____

____

Do you feel comfortable sharing these drawings with anyone? If so, who?

____

____

Cool-Down Tools: Things That Make Me Happy

You Need to Know

Thinking about things that make you happy can often help you when you are upset. By thinking about these things, your negative thoughts can change to positive thoughts. Some kids find it hard to think about happy things when they are upset. Using your "happy" feelings collage as a way of remembering the things that make you happy can help you to cool down.

Jamie was having a bad day. He thought he was going to his cousin's house to play, but his aunt called and said his cousin was sick. Jamie then asked Mom if they could go to the toy store, and Mom said, "maybe." Jamie didn't like when Mom couldn't give him a definite answer. He also hated waiting around for Mom to make up her mind. His dad was on the computer, and nothing was on TV that he wanted to watch. In Jamie's mind, everything was going wrong and there was nothing right. Jamie's Mom reminded him that he had made a "happy" feelings collage a while back. She had helped him find pictures of things he liked. She asked him to find the collage and to look at it for a while. While looking at it, Jamie began to smile. Here was a picture of everything he liked to do! It reminded Jamie that he liked to look at and to play with the cards he was collecting. Jamie was so unhappy that day that he had forgotten that he liked to do that! It also reminded Jamie that he liked to play with his pet hamster.

Sometimes changing what you are thinking about while you are upset can help calm you down. Looking at pictures of things that make you happy helps you to think about these things and can switch your thinking to more positive thoughts.

Activity 25

Cool-Down Tools: Things That Make Me Happy

Directions

Take out your "happy" feelings collage from Activity 4.

List some of the things that make you happy.

____

____

____

____

____

____

____

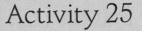

Take Note

Thinking about happy things can change your negative feelings to positive ones. Did this happen when you looked at your collage and made the list?

Yes __________ No __________

If yes, good for you! You can memorize what is on your collage so that you can see it in your imagination when you're upset and don't have the collage with you.

If no, use a different cool-down tool.

Activity 26 Become a Detective

You Need to Know

Knowing how people around you are feeling is important because it helps you know how to act with them. When people know that you are paying attention to how they are feeling, it makes them feel like you want to be with them.

Jacob and Bart sat at the same table in school. One day, Bart came into school looking sad. Jacob noticed that Bart was quiet and that he wasn't smiling as much as he usually did. Jacob asked Bart if something was wrong. Bart said that his cat was sick and he was sad and worried about her. Bart was glad that someone had asked him what was wrong, and he was able to play with Jacob and get his mind off of his cat for a while.

Directions

Become a detective. To practice knowing how your friends might be feeling, it will be your job to watch and notice how people in your family act. You need to watch and notice things about your family without them knowing what you are doing.

First look these questions over and then watch for the answers. You can answer the questions with information about anyone you observe. You can write the answers below.

Notice something that makes someone in your family happy. What was it? How did you know the person was happy? What did his or her face and body look like when they were happy? After you've written your answers, ask the person if he or she was feeling the way you thought and why. This will help you become a good detective.

For example, Pam was watching her mom. This is what she wrote:

> My mom was happy when she got a phone call. I could tell she was happy because she smiled and laughed while talking. She sat in a chair and looked comfortable. When I asked her later if she had been happy, she said she was because her sister called with good news.

Question 1

Notice something that makes someone in your family happy. What was it? How did you know the person was happy? What did his or her face and body look like when he or she was happy?

____

____

____

Ask the person if he or she was feeling the way you had thought he or she was feeling and why.

- ☐ I got it right! I can go on to the next question.
- ☐ Oops, I guessed wrong! I can try again.

Question 2

Notice something that makes someone in your family angry. What was it? How did you know the person was angry? What did his or her face and body look like when he or she was angry?

____

____

____

Ask the person if he or she was feeling the way you thought and why.

- ☐ I got it right! I can go on to the next question.
- ☐ Oops, I guessed wrong! I can try again.

Question 3

Notice something that makes someone in your family sad. What was it? How did you know the person was sad? What did his or her face and body look like when he or she was sad?

____

____

____

Ask the person if he or she was feeling the way you thought and why.

- ☐ I got it right! I can go on to the next question.
- ☐ Oops, I guessed wrong! I can try again.

Question 4

Notice something that makes someone in your family surprised. What was it? How did you know the person was surprised? What did his or her face and body look like when he or she was surprised?

___

___

___

Ask the person if he or she was feeling the way you thought and why.

- ☐ I got it right! I can go on to the next question.
- ☐ Oops, I guessed wrong! I can try again.

Take Note

If you got lots of the questions right in this activity, good for you! Now that you have practiced this at home, you can make guesses about what other people are feeling at school and in other places in your life.

If this was very difficult for you, keep practicing. Ask adults who care about you for help with this. Learning how to understand someone else's feelings and thoughts just by looking at them is a very difficult skill to learn. It's important to get this right at home first where it's okay to make mistakes and you can ask for help.

After you've practiced being a detective at home, try the following:

- Practice being a detective next time you are in the supermarket with your mom or dad.
- Practice being a detective next time you and your family go to visit other relatives.
- Practice being a detective next time you go on vacation.

Learn to Be a Mind Reader! Activity 27

You Need to Know

Some people can guess what other people feel and think very easily. For others, this is difficult. The good news is that you can learn to do this. But always remember, it's just a guess. Guessing what other people think and feel can help you to get along with others better.

Story 1

Ryan is playing a game that he loves with his friend Billy. Ryan looks up and sees Billy looking away and not paying attention to the game. Ryan guesses that Billy is bored and might want to play something else. He asks Billy if he'd like to continue this game or switch to something else. Billy feels happy that Ryan noticed how he was feeling and makes a suggestion to make things better. Billy feels able to tell Ryan what he wants to do.

Story 2

Tracy notices that her friend Isabelle is not playing with her at recess. Tracy asks Isabelle if she wants to go on the swing, and Isabelle just walks away without answering. Tracy guesses from Isabelle's behavior that Isabelle is angry with her. How does Tracy know this? Isabelle is one of Tracy's best friends, and Tracy knows that when Isabelle ignores her, something is wrong. Tracy can then ask Isabelle what is wrong, and they will have the chance to talk and work things out.

Learn to Be a Mind Reader!

Directions

Fill in answers to the questions below:

Scenario 1: Two boys are playing a board game.

What is the accused boy thinking?

____

____

____

____

____

____

Scenario 2: A group of kids are in the playground with Jim. Lots of the kids decide to play tag. Jim wanders away as the other kids begin their game.

What do the other kids think about Jim's behavior?

____

____

____

____

____

____

Scenario 3: Four kids are playing monopoly. One of the kids lands on Free Parking and goes to take the money on the board. Beth becomes very angry because she doesn't agree with the Free Parking rule that everyone else seems to know. Beth makes it impossible for the game to continue because she is angry and wants the money put back.

What are the other kids thinking?

____

____

____

____

____

____

Scenario 4: Kyle walks over to a small group of kids and begins to talk about Star Wars. The other kids roll their eyes, look away, and don't speak back.

What are the other kids thinking?

____

____

____

____

____

____

Take Note

Were you able to notice what a friend was feeling or thinking when you were spending time together?

Yes __________ No __________

If no, you can go back to practicing being a detective with your family or with a counselor who can help you learn how to do this. Learning to do this takes lots of practice!

If yes, write about what happened when you used the information you noticed.

____

____

____

____

____

____

____

____

____

____

____

By Accident? Or on Purpose!

Activity 28

You Need to Know

When it's difficult for you to guess what other people are thinking and feeling, it can also be confusing to know whether someone did something by accident or on purpose.

Sam is walking down the school hallway, and Jason bumps into him so hard that Sam drops his books. Sam becomes angry thinking that Jason did this on purpose. Jason, meanwhile, was daydreaming while walking down the hall and didn't see Sam. How could Sam know this?

If Sam could take a moment before reacting, he could look at Jason to see what his reaction is. Is Jason laughing? Is Jason surprised? Does Jason keep walking as if nothing happened? Sam might be able to get some helpful information from looking at Jason. If Sam is still confused, he can ask Jason: "Why did you do that?"

Directions

Look at the following comic strips. Look for clues that might help you decide if the actions shown were done by accident or on purpose.

Scenario 1: John goes to sit at his seat in school. When he sits down—"Ouch!"—he sits on a tack. There's a group of kids behind him—one kid is pointing; the others are laughing

Do you think the kids did this to John on purpose?

Yes ___________ No ___________

How did you come up with your answer? What are the clues you used?

____

____

____

Scenario 2: Sarah goes to sit with a group of kids in the lunchroom. Just as she gets to an empty seat, Jessica sits down in that seat.

Do you think Jessica did this to Sarah on purpose?

Yes ___________ No ___________

How did you come up with your answer? What are the clues you used?

____

____

____

Take Note

When Jessica took Sarah's seat, Sarah thought that Jessica did it on purpose. She thought that because Jessica seemed to rush over to the seat as if she were racing Sarah. Jessica, actually, was worried that she wouldn't be able to sit with the girls she liked to have lunch with so she rushed to the seat and didn't even see Sarah. A lunch monitor saw this and could tell that Jessica didn't see Sarah by noticing where Jessica was looking and what she was focused on. A friend of Sarah's thought that Jessica did it on purpose because the day before, Jessica told Sarah that she couldn't play tag with her friends at recess. The lunch monitor and Sarah's friend saw this differently. Sarah's friend knew what had happened the day before and the lunch monitor didn't. On the other hand, maybe Jessica really didn't see Sarah.

Can you see how complicated this can be?

Trying to figure out if someone did something to you on purpose or by accident can be difficult. While you are practicing this, it is a good idea to ask for help from someone safe who might be watching to see if what you think is correct. Two people can watch the same thing happen and disagree.

Activity 29

It All Depends on the Setting

You Need to Know

Rules change depending on where you are and who you are with. This is important to know so that you can ask questions to make sure the rules are what you think they are.

How could doing something be okay in one place and not be okay in another? Isn't a rule always a rule? WELL, NOT ALWAYS!! Think about it:

Ella likes to chew gum and her mom allows her to do this at home. When Ella chewed gum at school, she got in trouble with the teacher. Why? Because in Ella's school, gum chewing is not allowed.

Can you think of things that are okay to do and say at home but not in school?

Can you think of things that are okay to do and say at your grandparents' or other relative's house but not at home?

Can you think of things that are okay to do and say at a friend's house but not at home?

Can you think of things that are okay to do and say at home but not anywhere else?

Take Note

You should talk your answers over with an adult. There are lots of different situations when you have to think about the rules and if they apply. Some actions can be okay when you're with one person and not okay with another. An example of this would be that you hug and kiss your mom when you see her, but you wouldn't hug and kiss your teacher when you see her.

Can you think about a time that you got upset about a rule that you thought was being broken but in fact didn't apply to the setting or person?

____

____

____

____

Next time you find yourself getting upset about a rule you think should be followed, take a minute, use a cool-down tool, and see if you can ask some questions of people around you to see if the rule applies, and if it doesn't, why not?

Should I Tell? Activity 30

You Need to Know

Figuring out if you should tell on someone when you think they have broken a rule is difficult. Some kids see it as their job to report rule breaking anywhere, anytime. This can make it hard for them to have friends.

Some kids find it very hard not to tell on someone who breaks a rule.

There are many different kinds of rules:

- Game-playing rules (no cheating, take turns)
- School rules (no talking, no chewing gum)
- Social rules (saying "please" and "thank you," covering your mouth when you cough)
- Family rules (no TV before bed, show your parents your homework when it is finished)
- Legal rules (stop the car at a red light, don't steal)

When you see someone breaking a rule, think about the following questions:

1. Is anyone in danger?
2. Are you watching someone break a rule while they are doing something that doesn't involve you?
3. Are you involved with the person who is breaking the rule (for example, playing a game with them)?

These are suggestions for how to deal with the above questions:

1. If someone is in danger, you should tell a grown-up quickly.
2. If someone is breaking a rule that doesn't involve you and no one is in danger, don't tell.

3. If someone is breaking a rule while playing with you or bothering or teasing you, you can calmly ask them to stop. If they don't stop, you can stop playing with them, walk away, or ask an adult for help.

There is a difference between telling and tattling.

TELLING is when you tell on someone for the purpose of protecting someone else or yourself.

TATTLING is when you tell on someone for the purpose of getting them in trouble.

Should I Tell?

Activity 30

Directions

Look at the following cartoons and write if you would tell or not and why:

Scenario 1: One child calling another child names

Tell ________ Not tell ________

Why?

____

____

____

____

Scenario 2: Someone is passing a note while the teacher is writing on the blackboard.

Tell ________ Not tell ________

Why?

____

____

____

____

Scenario 3: You see a kid running into the street as traffic is coming. The adult present has their back turned.

Tell ________ Not tell ________

Why?

____

____

____

____

Take Note

Tell about a time where you told on someone and you thought it was the right thing to do:

____

____

____

Now that you've done the above activity, can you tell if what you did was...

"telling" ____________ or "tattling" ____________?

How can you tell which it was?

____

____

____

Do you enjoy seeing someone else get in trouble?

Yes ____________ No ____________

Why?

____

____

____

If your answer was "yes," you need to know that this is probably getting in the way of having friends. Other kids don't like it when someone enjoys tattling and getting kids in trouble.

Activity 31

Games: Winning and Losing

You Need to Know

Anytime two or more people play a game, one person will win and at least one person will lose. Being a good winner and a good loser are very important friendship skills.

Story 1

Gigi and Gabe were playing checkers. They both wanted to win very badly. Gigi won the game. Gabe was so angry and disappointed that he threw the game board across the room. Gigi was a little scared and knew that she would never play a game with Gabe again.

Story 2

Mandy and Mark were playing a card game. Mark had never played this game before, and Mandy told him she would help him learn. When it was clear that Mandy was going to win, she began to gloat, which means she made such a big deal about being ahead that she made Mark feel bad. Mark walked away to play with someone else.

Story 3

Ben and Danielle were playing a board game. At different times during the game they were each ahead, and it was hard to tell who would win. When Ben won, he smiled and said, "Good game!" to Danielle, because he had enjoyed the game. Danielle, though disappointed, said, "Good game!" too, because she realized she had enjoyed the game too. Ben and Danielle decided to play the game again.

This is how to be a "good" winner:

- Avoid gloating, because this makes others feel bad or mad.
- Tell the other person that you enjoyed playing the game.

This is how to be a "good" loser:

- Even if you are mad about losing, try to remain calm.
- Remember that you may have lots of chances to win in the future.
- See if you can learn something about winning the game by how the winner played.

Directions

Look at the following cartoons and fill in the blank lines.

What would the winner say to be a "good winner"? What might she be thinking?

____

____

____

____

____

____

What would the loser say to be a "good loser"? What might she be thinking?

____

____

____

____

____

____

Take Note

Nobody likes to lose! But if you want to play with other kids, you need to get used to losing. It's a good idea to practice how to be a "good loser" by playing games with people in your family. Sometimes practicing by playing a very quick game that you can play over and over (like tic-tac-toe) makes it easier, since you have lots of chances to win and lose. Kids who won't play games because they might lose are missing out on the fun and losing out on chances to make and keep friends.

Everybody likes to win. If you want to play with other kids, you need to do this gracefully. That means you shouldn't make the other person feel bad by making a really big deal about winning or saying mean things to the loser.

When you win or lose, you can keep any thoughts you have that might upset the other person to yourself.

Activity 32 Friendship Equations

You Need to Know

Your behavior with other kids either increases your chances of making friends or decreases your chances of making friends.

When someone tells on others a lot or tells them what to do or not to do, others get annoyed. This makes it hard to have friends. If you are telling only to get the person in trouble because they did something you didn't like or that was annoying to you, then chances are that person is going to be mad at you, even though you think you are right. Some kids think that being right is what's really important in a situation like this. But what they can't see is that they are choosing the rules over friendship.

The social cost is how other kids think and feel about you after you have behaved in a certain way and whether they want to be with you or not.

Friendship Equations

Activity 32

Below are some friendship equations that add some behaviors together to show the social cost of behaving in certain ways.

Being bossy about the rules
+ Not listening to how your friend wants to play

= Friend becoming annoyed and not wanting to play

Calmly discussing the rules
+ Compromising about the rules

= Friend wanting to play

Having to go first in a game all the time
+ Not giving your friends a chance to be first

= Friend not wanting to play

Taking turns even when you want to go first
+ Staying calm and not getting upset

= Friend wanting to play

Insisting on only playing the game you are interested in
+ Not thinking about what your friend wants to play

= (Fill in the answer) ____________________

Playing games that your friends want to play that aren't your favorite
+ Showing interest and playing to the end of the game

= (Fill in the answer) ____________________

Checking the rules a lot during the game
+ Not listening to what your friends say about the rules

= (Fill in the answer) ____________________

Directions

Try to write your own friendship equations. Write one that equals a friend wanting to play and one that equals a friend not wanting to play.

Take Note

List six things you can do that would help you make friends.

1. ______________________________
2. ______________________________
3. ______________________________
4. ______________________________
5. ______________________________
6. ______________________________

List six things you do that can hurt your chances of making friends.

1. ______________________________
2. ______________________________
3. ______________________________
4. ______________________________
5. ______________________________
6. ______________________________

Ask your parents to think about what they see you do when you are with other kids. Can they list some things you already do that help you make friends?

1. ______________________________
2. ______________________________
3. ______________________________
4. ______________________________

Ask your parents to think about what they see you do when you are with other kids. Can they list some things you do that hurt your chances of making friends?

1. ______________________________

2. ______________________________

3. ______________________________

4. ______________________________

You Need to Know

Kids who experience bullying and teasing need to learn ways to stay safe. Being aware of what is going on around you is an important skill to learn. This can help you avoid kids who can be mean.

In every school, there's a percentage of bullies, a percentage of victims, and a percentage of innocent bystanders, and this doesn't change from school to school. Why do you think this is?

In a school of one hundred children, how many do you think are bullies? ______

How many are victims? ______

And how many stand by and watch? ______

Actually, nine children would be bullies, eleven would be victims, and eighty would stand by and watch. This surprises lots of people! What do you think the eighty people do to avoid being picked on?

Most of the eighty are kids who are not often alone. They also are very aware of what is going on around them and who is near them, and they are good at guessing what other people are thinking and feeling. This helps them avoid the kids who can be mean. How do they know how to do this?

Some people have a natural talent for this. They are always "tuned in" to everything going on around them. Other people like to daydream. Their thoughts go to places in their imaginations. While it may feel good to be in that pretend place, being there makes it hard to really notice the world around you.

Directions

Circle the places and situations listed below where it is okay to daydream.

While playing at recess

In your classroom during math

In the lunchroom

In your room at home

At the dinner table

On a long trip in the car

While crossing the street

During your soccer game

While you are watching TV

While drawing a picture

While playing music

While eating breakfast

While your mom is telling you to get dressed for school

While walking down the hall at school

While getting changed for PE (teens)

While driving the car (teens)

While walking through a mall where there might be kids you know (teens)

While playing a card or a board game with your friends

While having a conversation with someone

Take Note

We want you to practice staying aware and paying attention to things that are going on around you.

Look at your family when you are together, at dinner for instance, and notice the following:

What is each person talking about?

____

____

What is each person doing?

____

____

List three other things about each person that you notice:

1. ____
2. ____
3. ____

1. ____
2. ____
3. ____

1. ____
2. ____
3. ____

(Get an extra piece of paper and add more sets of numbers if necessary.)

Activity 34 Friendship Connections

You Need to Know

Part of staying safe is to be with other people. Kids will want to spend time with you if you know how to have an interesting conversation with them.

When you know where and when to stay aware of what's going on around you, it's a good idea to be with other kids. This not only helps to keep you safe from teasing, it also helps you find friends who might have things in common with you. The way people find out if they have things in common with you is to have conversations.

When you are talking to someone else or a group of people, it is helpful to think of the different ways you might do this. You can think of a conversation being like a tennis match. One person speaks (hits the ball) to another person, who answers or speaks (hits the ball back), and it goes back and forth. They are both involved, and it is a good game. If a tennis player is not watching (listening) and loses track of the ball (doesn't pay attention to what the other person is saying), they miss the ball and lose a point. If there are four people playing in a tennis match, they all want turns to get into the game and hit the ball (get their part of the conversation in).

A basic way to think about the different ways people can talk is to think of the following three types of talk

Friendly Talk

This type of talk includes both people having a conversation with lots of listening, questioning, turn taking, and showing interest in each other by looking at each other.

Talk for Yourself

This type of talk is when there are two people speaking but only one person is talking a lot. The person who is talking is not showing much interest in the other person and isn't looking at the person or noticing if that person is bored or interested.

Talk to Yourself

This type of talk is when you say something to yourself, either silently to yourself in your head or out loud to yourself. It is best, if you are saying it out loud, to do this while you are by yourself. Other people might think it is strange and confusing to see you talk out loud to yourself when you are around other people.

Directions

Think about the different types of talking and draw a picture of one type.

Take Note

For some people it is very difficult to stop talking about a subject that is stuck in their head. They feel a real need to finish what they are saying, but it goes on for so long that it leaves the other person out of the conversation. If you find it difficult to stop talking you may want to:

- Try to finish the thought silently in your head
- Write it down
- Talk about it later

Ask your parents or other adults who know you well to help you with the following:

On the scale below, rate yourself for how often you use Friendly Talk with kids:

1 2 3 4 5 6 7 8 9 10

Never Sometimes Always

On the scale below, rate yourself for how often you use Talking for Yourself with kids:

1 2 3 4 5 6 7 8 9 10

Never Sometimes Always

On the scale below, rate yourself for how often you use Talking to Yourself when you are with other kids:

1 2 3 4 5 6 7 8 9 10

Never Sometimes Always

Activity 35 Deciding Who to Play With

You Need to Know

You may be like lots of kids who want to be friends with the popular kids. What you really want to look for are kids who want to be friends with you and who treat you nicely. These people may be the popular kids or they may not be.

Ever since the beginning of the school year, Caitlin wanted to be friends with Joy, Madison, and Cara. They always looked like they were having fun. All the kids in Caitlin's grade seemed to want to be with these girls. When Caitlin tried to play with them at recess, they ignored her. One day Caitlin heard Madison say to her friends that Caitlin was a baby. This upset Caitlin, but she thought that she should just try harder to make them her friends. The harder Caitlin tried, the meaner the girls became. After discussing this with her mom, Caitlin looked around at all the girls in her grade and realized that Maya and Jackie were playing on the swings, Caitlin's favorite place at recess. She decided to approach Maya and Jackie to see if she could play with them. They did not ignore her, they did not call her names, and they asked her to stay with them. They even asked her to have lunch with them the next day!

We call kids who are friendly and treat you nicely "safe kids." The kids who might tease, bully or ignore you, we call "unsafe kids." In this story, Maya and Jackie were "safe kids" for Caitlin, while Madison, Joy, and Cara weren't. By learning this, Caitlin made new friends.

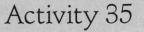

Directions

1. Make a list of kids you know.

____________________	____________________
____________________	____________________
____________________	____________________
____________________	____________________
____________________	____________________

2. Look at this list that describes the behavior of safe and unsafe kids.

   Safe

   1. Greets you when he or she sees you
   2. Asks you to play
   3. Helps you when you need help
   4. Shares with you
   5. Takes turns playing what you want to play some of the time

   Unsafe

   1. Teases you or calls you names
   2. Tries to hurt you physically
   3. Laughs at you and gets other kids to laugh at you
   4. Ignores you
   5. Bosses you around

3. Next to the name of each kid you listed above, put a check mark for every safe behavior and an "x" next to every unsafe behavior.

4. Look this list of kids over with a grown-up and talk about who might be the best choices for you.

Take Note

Look back at the list of kids you made. Do you see more checks or x's? If you see mostly checks, it seems that you are doing a good job of choosing safe friends. If you see more x's, you may need to come up with a new plan for finding safe friends. Here are some suggestions of what you can do:

- Look around at all the kids you can play with, even ones that you may not have been interested in before.
- Notice the kids' behavior and look for kids who are acting in safe ways (look at the list on the last page).
- Try playing with these kids and see which ones are the kindest.
- Remember that it's not important how popular a kid is when you are thinking of reasons to choose a friend, it's how they treat you that is important.

If you have a hard time finding safe kids, ask your parents, teacher, or counselor for help. They may be able to point out some safe kids who you can play with.

Friendship Solar System

Activity 36

You Need to Know

There are different levels of friendship. When you know the level of friendship that you have with someone, it's easier to know what to expect from them and what they expect from you.

Story 1

A new boy, Marcel, came into Curt's class one day. Curt was very excited about this because he didn't have many friends and thought that Marcel could be his best friend. Curt followed Marcel at lunchtime and recess and tried to talk to him as much as he could during class. At first, Marcel was glad to meet someone so friendly. After a while, however, Marcel found Curt's behavior annoying because he didn't give Marcel a chance to get to know and play with the other kids. Marcel thought it was strange that Curt would try to act like his best friend so quickly, because he knew that friendships take a long time to develop.

Story 2

Alexa stays to herself at school. She eats lunch by herself and stands at the edge of the yard at recess. The other kids don't know why Alexa stays by herself, but after asking her to play a few times and having her say no, they leave Alexa alone. When Alexa's mom asks her who she would like to invite to her birthday party, Alexa names all the girls in her class. Alexa is surprised and upset when none of the girls want to come. She thought they were all her friends. The girls find out that Alexa is upset about this and they are surprised because they did not think Alexa was interested in being friends with them. The girls know that if you want to be friends, you need to show that in your behavior by playing together. They thought they would feel strange to attend a birthday party for someone they hardly know.

Most kids have one or two friends they are very close with (best friends), a few kids that they know and like and play with sometimes (friends), and lots of kids who they just know (acquaintances).

To help yourself understand the levels of friends in your life, draw a friendship solar system where you are the sun, the closest ring around you will show your best friends, the next ring your friends, and the last ring your acquaintances. See the example below to help you with your drawing.

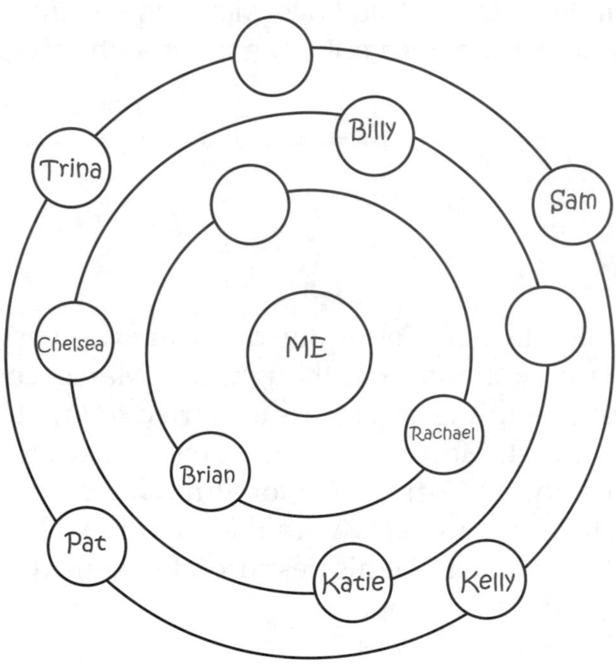

Take Note

Now that you have completed your friendship solar system, look at the following definitions of different levels of friendship and see if you put your friends on the correct levels.

What does it mean to be a best friend? Usually, best friends:

- Spend lots of time together
- Talk about things they are both interested in
- Trust each other (this usually happens over time)
- Ask each other for help
- Are happy for each other when good things happen
- Cheer each other up when bad things happen

What does it mean to be a friend? Usually, friends:

- Spend some time together
- Talk about things they are both interested in
- Play in groups together
- Are kind to each other

What does it mean to be an acquaintance?

- You know the person's name.
- You are friendly when you see each other.
- You might play or talk together once in a while.

Show your drawing to your parents and/or to the adult who gave you this book so that they can help you make sure that your friendship solar system is accurate.

Activity 37 Do You Get Stuck?

You Need to Know

Some kids are very flexible and can move from one activity to another very easily, can stop a thought in their head from repeating itself, and can talk about many different subjects. Other kids need to learn how to do these things, as they become "stuck." When you are "stuck," it's hard for people to be with you.

The term "stuck" is used to describe:

- When you have a thought in your head and can't stop thinking about it
- When you want to talk about a certain subject and can't stop talking about it
- When something unexpected happens and you need to change your plan, but you can't let go of the old plan

In all these cases, remaining stuck makes it difficult to be with people or for them to want to be with you. They don't understand why you don't get "unstuck," because most people can do this pretty easily.

Patrick is playing his video game when his mom interrupts him unexpectedly and says they have to leave to go to the store. While Patrick doesn't want to stop playing, he knows he'll have a chance to play later or tomorrow so he switches off the game and gets ready to go to the store. His brother, Alex, on the other hand is watching his favorite video when his mother announces this new plan and he gets stuck. He refuses to turn off the TV, and when his mother does it for him, he melts down. When, eventually, they are on their way to the store, Alex cannot stop talking about what he was watching, even though his mother and Patrick are not interested in this topic.

Do you get stuck?

Yes—If you do, describe how and where you get stuck.

____

____

____

____

____

____

____

____

____

____

No—If you think you don't get stuck, ask a grown-up who knows you well (your parents, counselor, or teacher) if they think you get stuck and how (have them give you some examples).

Fill in the comic strip below showing what happens when you get stuck.

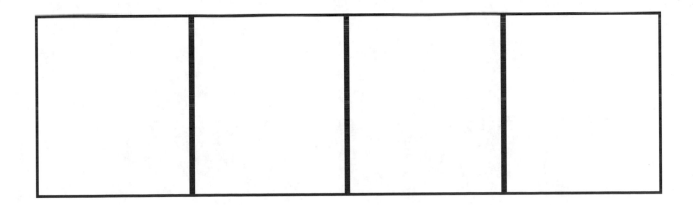

Take Note

The first step in learning how to get unstuck is to be aware that you are stuck. This is difficult to do on your own. You may need your parents and other grown-ups you trust to help you. They can just tell you that you're stuck, or together you can come up with a code word or gesture that means "you are stuck," so that they can let you know about this without having to actually say it.

What code word or gesture do you think would work for you?

____

____

____

____

Once someone says the code word or uses the gesture, your job is to work on getting unstuck. Using cool-down tools works for some kids so that they can relax enough to try new behaviors. The next activity will give you some suggestions on how to do this.

How to Get "Unstuck"

Activity 38

You Need to Know

Having the ability to get unstuck when you are with other kids will make it easier for you to focus on them. This is a key skill for building friendships.

Farmer Bill has a wheelbarrow that he uses to bring seeds down a narrow path to a patch of land at the back of his farm. Since Farmer Bill takes the same path every day to bring the seeds to that patch, his wheelbarrow has created a rut in the ground. Farmer Bill notices that he's getting slower everyday. The rut has gotten so deep that it slows the wheelbarrow down and makes it hard to get to where he wants to go. He decides to try to push the wheelbarrow down the path next to the rut and finds that the wheel gets drawn down into the same old rut. It's hard and frustrating for Farmer Bill to create new paths and he has to work very hard to focus on keeping the wheelbarrow from getting stuck in the old rut.

If we think of Farmer Bill's road like a brain, and the wheelbarrow like your thoughts, you can see how difficult it can be to stop being stuck and to create something new.

If you were able to figure out when and how you get stuck in the last exercise, then these are some things that might help you get unstuck:

- Stay aware of times when you may be getting stuck and say to yourself, "I am stuck."
- Create a picture of something getting unstuck. (For the story above, we used a wheelbarrow making a new path.) Draw a picture or an icon of how you can imagine getting unstuck.
- Use this image to help you get unstuck. Think of it whenever you might be stuck, or when someone tells you that you are stuck.

For example, see the comic strip below.

Directions

Draw your icon or image of "unstuck" here. After you draw your icon, make a copy of it to keep with you in your pocket or in your book bag as a reminder to pay attention to when you are stuck and to remember how to get unstuck.

  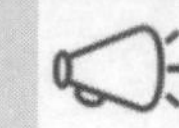

Take Note

Learning how to become unstuck can be difficult and can take lots of time and practice. Many kids become stuck because they are nervous, and they may not even know why. Practicing the cool-down tools that worked for you and paying attention to your feelings will help you with this. So will using your icon.

Just as Farmer Bill, in the example above, needed patience to create a new pathway, so do you. You are actually helping your brain to work in a different way, a way that will help you to get unstuck and that will make it easier for you to have friends. This can take time.

What's Changed About Me?

Activity 39

You Need to Know

Now that you have come to the end of this book, it's a good idea for you to think about your strengths and weaknesses again. This way you can see how far you've come.

When Carmen did her drawing about her strengths and weaknesses earlier in this book, she realized that one of her weaknesses was not being good at recess. After doing the activities in this book, Carmen worked on paying attention to what was going on around her by watching the other kids' facial expressions and body language. Because she did this, Carmen was able to focus on what the other kids were doing and join in. Carmen was very happy to see that she had successfully worked on her weakness.

What's Changed About Me?

Directions

Look back at Activity 15 to see what you thought your strengths and weaknesses were when you began this book. Has anything changed? Because you have been working on knowing yourself and knowing others, it is important to check in with yourself to see what, if anything, has changed about you. Draw a picture about what has changed below. If you have trouble thinking about this, please ask an adult who knows you well to help you. That person might see new areas you've successfully worked on that are hard for you to see.

Take Note

How do you feel about the changes you see in yourself?

Do your parents see these changes?

Do your friends see these changes?

Activity 40 You've Done It!

You Need to Know

It's important to spend some time thinking about the progress you've made and the things you may still need to work on. By completing this book, you've taken an important step in Knowing Yourself and Knowing Others!

Improving your friendship skills by knowing more about yourself and knowing how to make and keep friends is hard work! We know from working with lots of kids that change takes time, can be frustrating, and can also be rewarding. We also know that all kids can always learn more skills to help make friendships easier. We hope we have made the activities fun for you.

You've Done It!

Activity 40

To review, here are some of the skills you worked on by using this book:

- Getting better at knowing what you're feeling
- Getting better at letting people know what you're feeling
- Getting better at knowing what other people are feeling
- Getting better at dealing with disagreements with friends
- Understanding how your friends might be feeling
- Tolerating frustration better (with yourself or other people)
- Practicing conversation skills with one other person
- Starting a conversation
- Listening to what your friends want to say
- Practicing conversation skills with a group
- Getting better at dealing with disagreements with friends
- Allowing others to lead when playing or working in a group (learning how to be a team player)
- Getting better at winning and losing a game
- Getting better at changing the topic or plan, when you are really set on talking about or doing something
- Getting better at dealing with things that don't go the way you expect them to go (when the plan changes)

Directions

To help you know how much progress you've made, draw a picture of the following.

1. Here's something I learned from this workbook that has helped me to be a better friend.

2. Here's something I still need to work on to be a better friend.

Take Note

Pat yourself on the back! By this we mean that you should be very proud of yourself for completing this book. Giving yourself a pat on the back is like a message from you to you that says:

"GOOD JOB!"

Nancy Widdows, MS, ATR-BC, LPC, is a licensed professional counselor and registered, board-certified art therapist with thirteen years' experience treating children in school, hospital, and private practice settings. Widdows' specialty is using art therapy to create concrete visual tools to help kids understand the social environment. Cooper and Widdows co-direct SuperKids, a unique program that focuses exclusively on social skills development, in Ridgefield, Norwalk, and Orange, Connecticut.

Barbara Cooper, MPS, ATR-BC, LMHC, is a registered, board-certified art therapist with twenty-three years of experience treating children and adults in school, hospital, and private practice settings. Her specialty is helping parents develop their own style of effective parenting. With Widdows, she is co-director of SuperKids, a social skills program in Connecticut. Cooper received her master's degree in art therapy from the Pratt Institute in New York, where she is now an associate professor.

more instant help books

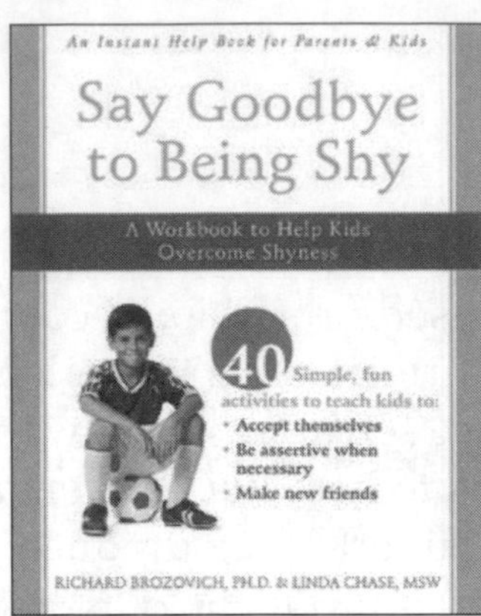

SAY GOODBYE TO BEING SHY

A Workbook to Help Kids Overcome Shyness

US $16.95 / ISBN: 978-1572246096

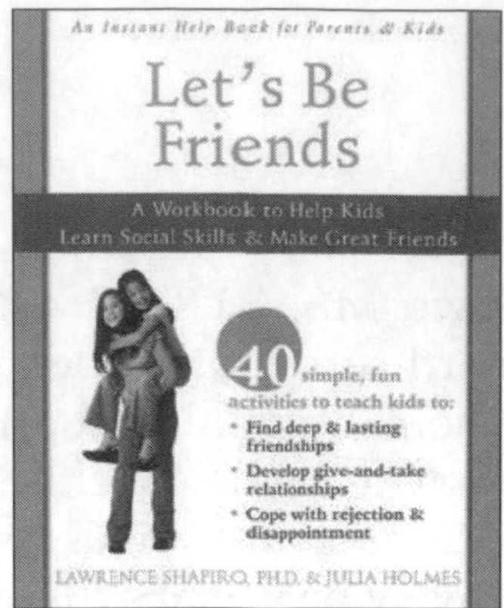

LET'S BE FRIENDS

A Workbook to Help Kids Learn Social Skills & Make Great Friends

US $16.95 / ISBN: 978-1572246102

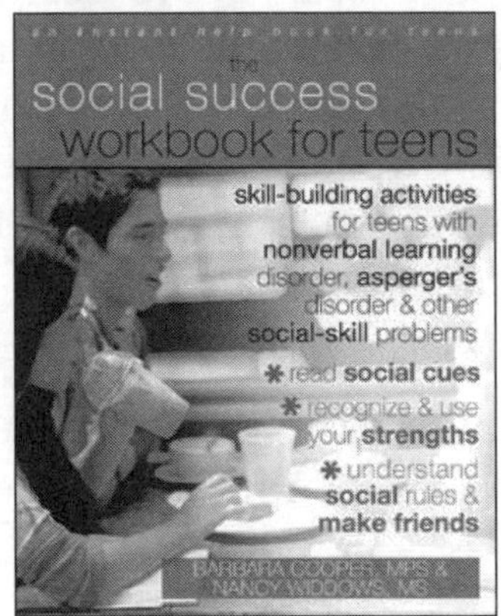

THE SOCIAL SUCCESS WORKBOOK FOR TEENS

Skill-Building Activities for Teens with Nonverbal Learning Disorder, Asperger's Disorder & Other Social-Skill Problems

US $14.95 / ISBN: 978-1572246140

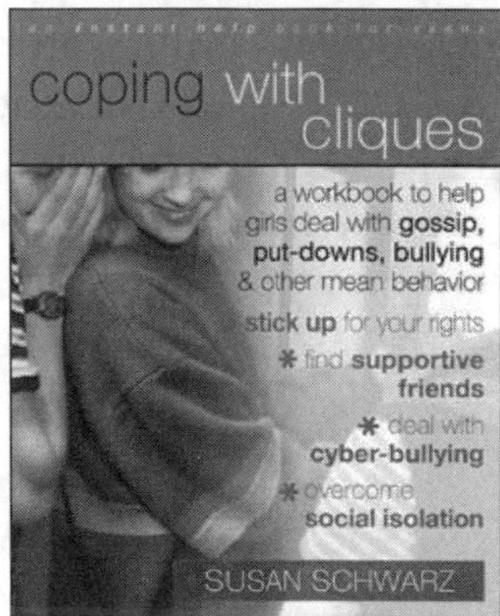

COPING WITH CLIQUES

A Workbook to Help Girls Deal with Gossip, Put-Downs, Bullying & Other Mean Behavior

US $14.95 / ISBN: 978-1572246133

available from

and fine booksellers everywhere

To order, call toll free **1-800-748-6273** or visit our online bookstore at **www.newharbinger.com**

(VISA, MC, AMEX / prices subject to change without notice)